With affection and sharp attention, LeCount celebrates ordinary loveliness. He writes with generous and twinkling consideration, and his readers will find in these lovely haiku a portrait of his town and its people, and a fondness and celebration for their world.

Lisa Allen Ortiz, poet and author of *Turns Out*

A collection of haiku which recommends its author by his gentle perspective towards his family, towards the inside and outside of his living space. David LeCount presents us with his clear heart and unfailing eye many details, forms and shapes, lights, colors and sounds of his landscape throughout the year, and leaves us lingering with his fresh poetical moments for our great delight.

Ion Codrescu, Romanian Haiku poet

LaHonda
Journal
a haiku diary

Author's Note

These poems/haiku were written after my family and I moved from the suburbs of Menlo Park to the town of La Honda in the Santa Cruz Mountains. Because this book is also a diary, the poems reflect not only what was happening in nature but also in my family and people close to it. I had hoped our children would have experiences with farm animals, with hiking in the woods, and with fishing in the rivers. In short, I wanted them to have many of the same experiences I had as a child living in a rural setting. So it was that we had geese, horses (Bess and Cinnamon), pigs (Bacon and Eggs), one Guernsey cow (Daisy), and countless nameless chickens. Probably the dearest, however, were our various large dogs (Harvey, Fred, Hannibal, Scammon and Shasta).

During this time, my family and I took trips to other countries. Trips to Japan, China, Hong Kong as well as parts of Europe gave me more love both for where I had been and where I lived. Flights to other countries as well as flights of imagination originated from La Honda, adventures took place there and from there and so I have entitled this book "La Honda Journal".

So it was that La Honda inspired me, and reminded me of other rural places where I had lived and learned to love nature: Lagunitas, California; Fort Washakie, Wyoming; Whately, Massachusetts and College, Alaska.

I call this book "a haiku diary" because
for the better part of forty years I have been
experimenting with what haiku could look like
in English based on my experience in nature as a
westerner.

> — *David E. LeCount*
> *Autumn, 2011*

LaHonda Journal

a haiku diary

by
David E. LeCount

Day's Eye Press and Studios
El Granada, California

Day'sEye Press and Studios
PO Box 628
El Granada, CA 94018
info@dayseyepressandstudios.com
www.dayseyepressandstudios.com

ISBN: 978-0-9619714-3-4

Printed in the United States of America

Cover photo and design copyright 2011
by Diane Lee Moomey

Introduction

Here is a stimulating collection of haiku by a poet who cherishes the venerable spirit and subtle aesthetic values of traditional haiku poetry. David LeCount has by his poems ennobled this genre, making it truly worthy of the phrase *traditional haiku poetry*, by which it has been known for centuries and is seldom known today.

LeCount's haiku are indeed poems: he is a skilled and informed poet and as an ardent student of Thoreau, he shares Thoreau's awareness of the Wild. Nature has been a vital part of LeCount's life as the wide variety of his subjects amply testify.

LeCount is a wordsmith and his poems, uniformly in three lines, are written with such care that the haiku moment is clearly revealed. This is no misbegotten attempt at minimalism: in these poems the sole emphasis is on that perfect Moment.

Life-fulness seems the very heart of LeCount's writings. His acuity of perception is phenomenal and at times awesome—one can but marvel at it. Such a Zen-centered awareness of the Eternal Now raises one's ken of life and ultimately of the true nature of reality itself.

Indeed, LeCount's keen perception displays a path of spiritual awareness. Such concentrated focus can have profound metaphysical consequences, not unlike the methodology of Zen meditation.

The abstractions of words and notions that fill and wander about the labyrinth of the thinking mind preclude awareness of life's quintessential Thusness. In the author's direct sensuous perception of life's Eternal Now is revealed the quintessential flow of the ever-changing nature of life and reality. And in this is presented a significant irony: that this the shortest form of poetry has the potential to center and raise human consciousness to the highest level, a level which is so badly needed today.

James W. Hackett, haiku poet and author of
Zen Haiku and Other Poems, The Way of Haiku, Bug Haiku, Haiku Poetry, volumes 1–4, and A Traveler's Haiku
21 September 2011

The Haiku

Come in her nightgown

to watch the moon—

I watch her...

From her rocking chair

she orders things done

with her knitting needle

Under the waterfall

she bathes her hair just to feel

its plummeting flow

A grass whistle:

bitter-pitched and withered

between thumb and breath

Lurking in my socks:

a foxtail or two

from last summer's hike

Winter desert—

a shed snakeskin threading

the wind between rocks

The yarn ball

unwinds with the speed

of the cat's attack!

Spring morning meadow—

to catch the goats demands

bounding as they do

Withered grass

the barn cat creeps lower

than her shoulders...

Large family brunch...
and first to the table
are the ants!

To write, the old waitress
takes the pencil behind her ear
and tongues the point

On daddy's shoulder
his daughter reaches the apple,
then pees warmly

Young girls — how gladly

they lift their skirts up

to model petticoats . . .

In mother's closet,

the chocolates are hidden

behind old shoes

Quiet Sunday until —

in stocking feet she finds

a jack on the floor!

An old wicker creel
still breathes of campfire smoke
and hidden mountain lakes

Wilderness trek—
every mosquito decides it too
must come along

Willows whip past the face
under the full moon—
still we gallop

Its bill packed with fish,

the pelican belly-flops

onto the salt-worn pier

Catching a frog

with only my cupped hands

for his pond...

Helping dig their wallow...

the piglets root around

and stand on my shovel

Autumn in the park...
the blind man feels a leaf
where his checker was

At midnight, a single dog bark
at the moon
perfects loneliness

Scrambling sideways—
yet the crab eyes before him
the incoming tide

In moonlight,
who dares feel for the dank side
of garden stones?

In the autumn path:
seven holes the picky squirrel
dug . . . and abandoned

Early autumn—
the mosquito warming himself on me
before he bites

On the radio:

lightning explodes in static

then summer silence

                 Bedtime—

          alone now, the child

         sucks his toothbrush

Grandmother's hair

almost to her elbows at night:

the gray she takes down

The sleeping rabbit—

its ears and nose

still keeping track

Rope swing—

bending and swaying, the willow

shapes the trip

Roosting at dusk,

the hen barely cares

who feels for eggs

Holding hands

in the rain...the warmth

that mingles drips

                Beware of her sigh!

          it roars from all the women

                who ever were...

Tie your sweater

around your waist...the mountain

has no path from here on!

Saying goodbye...the wind

blows your long hair

across your lips

This column of ants

repeats each detour though the leader

is long gone

Digging for "treasure"...

two boys hushed having found

a rusted square nail

Counting daisies—

then she counts shooting stars...

all there!

                     Unfamiliar beach—

                he lifts his leg to mark

                    territory...on me

Late in the fall sun—

a child's forgotten crayons

coloring alone

The feed store mouser

high above the hunt, sleeps

on sacks of Pig Chow

Autumn morning—

the garden spider's catch

a web of holes

The squirrel's daring:

down the oak tree

headfirst!

In his gentle palm
he holds the winners of
the first ever sow bug race

"How did you get up there?"
a child in the pine approves
of his father's wonder

Asleep in the field...
the grass awakes in my cheek
that warm itch of green

At the window pane—

a fly busily measuring

the jail he can't see

The ice cream man—

summer disappearing in bells

far down the street

To accompany

his flea scratching, a paw

must thump the porch

The old gloves
hold the same wrinkles worked
into my hands

                        Escaped mule
                ate the morning glories,
                    blue and all...

Enthusiastic boy—
blackberries staining on him
a clown's mouth

Fir shadows sinking
to the sunny stream bottom
weightlessly

Lingering solitude...
a fly walks the honeyed bottom
of a used coffee cup

Gentle autumn rain —
at its start my sleep deepens
into water

This soap bubble's skin
with my finger inside it
just will not pop

Beside the stream:
whatever makes her whisper
makes me too...

Her first locket...
in it a stranger's face
that comes with it

Washed ashore with the tide—
seagull bones give rise
to a cloud of flies

Old oak trunk—
the boy tries to hug it
just for its size

Creaking windmill:
the sound of ancient groans
bearing home water

In the stone fence

a young girl counts faces

of old women she knows

He licks his paws

and sighs...that his feet

weren't taken for a walk

For the toddler

who just learned to walk:

excited tiptoeing

Storing his toys
in the attic amid sighs
deep from her womb

Sea fog
dripping down the tombstones
slows on mossy letters

The young buck
scratching antler velvet off
strops the dead branch

Patrolling the clam bed,

the hungry sandpiper finds

all doors shut

Meditation

within the spider

tools the shape of its orb

The two year old—

above this mountain path

all birds are "eagles". . .

The "treasure"

he carried home: a toad

the highway flattened

Thinking of apples,

the toddler eats to the white core

of the strawberry

The chimney smoke

first drifts with the wind, then

becomes it

Behind the fence post,

a cat takes its noon nap

to a fatter shadow

Picture window —

a hummingbird stares at me

in my cage

Trudging through the sand —

now I know how heavy

this whole beach is...

The old quilt

shudders its stuffing

on grandma's shins

Two fine grandfathers

loved enough they don't mind

strolling arm and arm

Except for this fog,

an old lady's clothesline

hangs emptied

At my typewriter
the toddler spells all words
with the "j" key

              In the park swing
       the child's glee climbs to terror
              and back again

Scrubbing the kitchen table,
the old mother hesitates
over which son sat where

With the motor running

she stops to pick blackberries

in a red skirt!

"Naked ladies"

in the cemetery aisle—

that pink of baby gifts

Over the old bridge

he stomps the weathered slats

to startle the trolls away...

Stuck in the pig wallow
my foot comes out—but the boot
wades a little longer

Hidden in the moss:
now and then a frog's bubble
says he's home

The autumn rainstorm—
planned to plant her tulip bulbs
and plant she does!

Floating in the tea
the mint still tastes
of the cold garden

After three boys...
the mother cutting her steak
into bite-sized cubes

Dogprints in fireplace ash —
on this windy night
moon craters

A dry spring day...

the courage needed to thin

young carrots out

        Stranded on the beach—

          the one oar still rowing

            deep in the sand

An abandoned shoe

in the beach sand the waves

keep throwing away

The swallow's mud nest

not yet dry—and yet

she's sitting still

Lost in the sand,

my toes take on their own life

for just a moment

Summer solstice—

a sparrow burns its feet

on the sun-dial

Pounding rain—

in the stillest white the mushroom

is its own umbrella

Silent in the rain,

the cat licks wetness

off a paw

In the bear's footprints,

I walk the empty beach

not fitting in

Dark kitchen drawer—
a growing potato eye
startles her touch

Gently his fat weight
sinks the lily pad—yet,
the frog is himself

In her sleep
I am no one but the warmth
of another sheet

47

From beneath the car

the prosthetic hand

reaches for a wrench

Winter evening—

three people run to answer

one phone call

In the dripping heat

a cat basks in sunlight

still cold at the nose

Chinese market —
the old man with the flyswatter
sleeps on a rice sack

On the face
the swatted mosquito smudge
leaves its blood too

Rest home bus —
faces fly by fast
becoming ghosts

Spring woodpecker—
the sound of the telephone pole
echoes dew

        Needless loveliness—
    her flower arrangement dines
        with the widow

Rusting in his yard,
the seat stuffing of the car
grows morning glories

Pennies in the well—
the koi nibbles one
in its daily rounds

A forgetful horse
on the way out . . . but coming home
each short-cut known

Just one eye of the frog
rises above the surface
to share the dusk

The unspoken rule:

my dog will chase each new cat

to the gate, no farther

                    In the child's swing

            she sits...in one simple sway

                        girlhood returns

Meeting owl eyes

at dusk: knowing

for just a moment

Overlooked

as beach firewood: a log

still weighted with sea

To my watering

the old jay descends the fir

one branch at a time

Down the garden hose,

ants file from their flooded nest

portaging eggs

Hearing the brook...

when she is not there

I think of tiger lilies

        Four leaf clover—

        in this heat wilted

           into one leaf

One button missing!

my best shirt,

the last minute!

Country ballyard—
playing deep centerfield
a covey of quail

Climbing the rope ladder
to the tree fort:
wild roses

"Dueling" newspapers:
the old couple read to each other
without taking turns

Turtle's temple:

the island in the pond

where slow walking's safe

Browsing cows —

each tail swats flies

to the same rhythm

After the tractor

marches the crow inspecting

for mowed snakes

Mountain temple—
a flurry of pigeon wings showers
white on the monks below

Stumbling on a stone—
the drunk finds a path home
that wasn't there before

Startled from the oak,
a hive of monarchs gusts
into autumn leaves

On the moonlit shore —

a chill the wind left in stones

for me to walk on

A blind beggar...

the wind's voice across his cup

the height of his coins

Foggy rain —

cows to the pasture still leave

tracks of breath

A rainy beach...
all he finds to play with
seagull bones

Sewing by the stove...
the rain on the roof
soothes each stitch

The bug I untrap
from the scum of the pond
sticks to my finger

A father's pride:
sons who leave the front door open
just to hear the rain

A fish that size?
pelican, point your beak up
and shake it on down

Autumn rain—
each patter in the gutter
makes a leaf dance

Hopping over the puddle,

I hop over

the woodland sky

In the child's swing

she murmurs, "run under me"

to the rising breeze

The heron at dawn —

its shadow stands folded

in prayer for frogs

Autumn sunrise—

a weed he lifts his leg on

crackles like fire

Children on the bridge

whisper so the trolls beneath

cannot hear

Autumn wind—

nothing left on the oak

for winter to take

The fog

lifting lightly her veil:

the widowed nun

The wild pear tree...

under its leaves

droops the moon

Petting the lizard

the child puts to sleep

its leathery thorns

A soaring hawk

rose -colored at that height:

the sun through its blood

      Measuring out two cords:

      the woodsman walks it off

         with his ax handle

Long brown hair—

in her braids the sun

weaves such shine

DAVID E. LECOUNT received a BA in English from the University of Alaska in Fairbanks and an MFA in Creative Writing from the University of Massachusetts in Amherst. He is the recipient of an NEA Creative Writing Fellowship.

He received a Grand Prize from the Modern Haiku Society of Japan for his poetry and has addressed the World Haiku Festival in the town of Leeuwarden, the Netherlands.

His prize-winning haiku have been published in Japan, USA, China, England and Romania and, to his delight, occasionally appear on bottles of tea in the USA and in Japan.

After teaching high school English for over thirty years, LeCount now contents himself with tutoring in English and elementary Chinese. He is the author of two books on the teaching of writing, ***Nonstandardized Quests*** and ***Dream Writing Assignments***, and has been a consultant for Stanford University's Center for Educational Research. His teaching has received awards including an Inspirational Teacher Award from UC Santa Cruz, and a Dorothy Wright Teaching Award from San Jose State University.

LeCount is currently enjoying his (semi) retirement with his family, pets, and assorted wildlife in La Honda, California, a rural community in the Santa Cruz mountains south of San Francisco.

You can write to him at dleco@batnet.com.